CONCERT PIECE

for **Solo Alto** or **Tenor** or **Baritone Saxophone**
or **Trumpet (Cornet)** or **Trombone** or **Baritone** or **Tuba**
and **Symphonic Band**

Duration : 4′ ca

VACLAV NELHYBEL

8500

© Copyright 1973 by E. C. KERBY Ltd., Toronto
International Copyright Secured

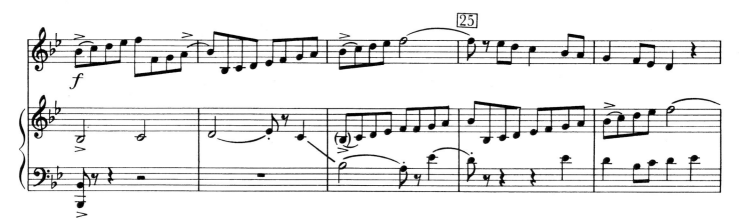

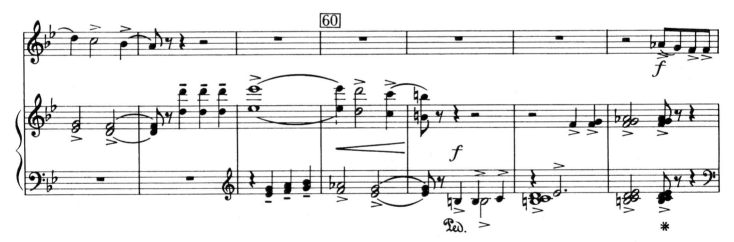

CONCERT PIECE

for **Solo Alto** *or* **Tenor** *or* **Baritone Saxophone**
or **Trumpet (Cornet)** *or* **Trombone** *or* **Baritone** *or* **Tuba**
and **Symphonic Band**

Duration : 4′ ca

VACLAV NELHYBEL

Trombone
Baritone (B.C.)

Allegro marcato

8816

© Copyright 1973 by E. C. KERBY Ltd., Toronto
International Copyright Secured

Più vivo

mf

145 **Molto vivo**

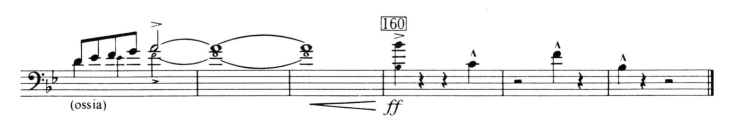

(ossia)

ff

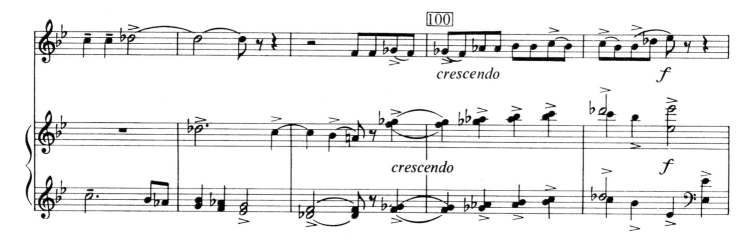

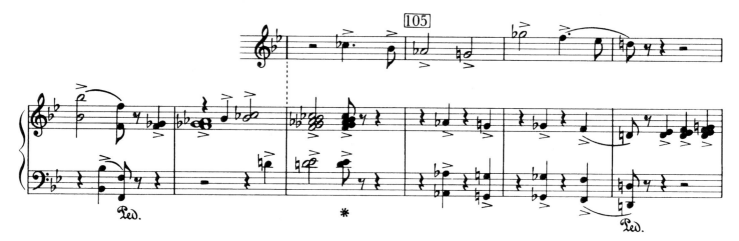

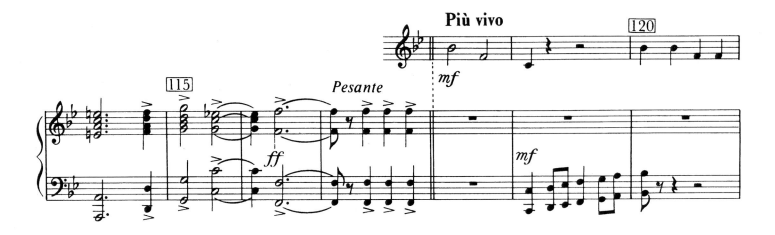

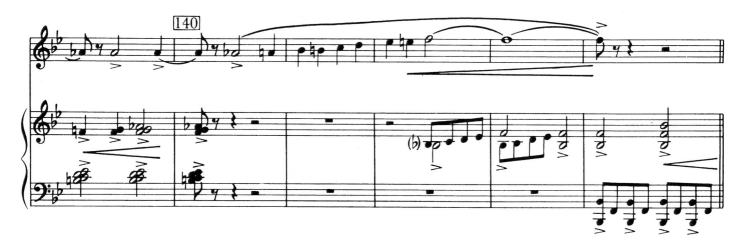

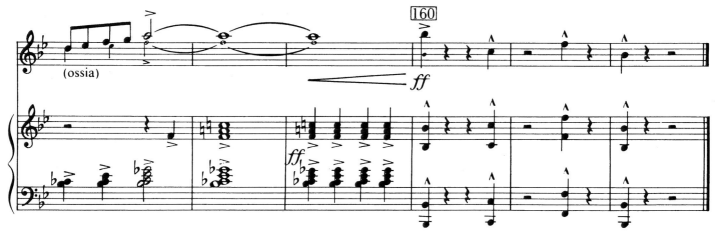